# Goose, Moose, and Mongoose

## by Dave Miller, Ph.D.

A.P. "Learn to Read" Series

God made the goose.

The goose is a bird.

The goose can fly.

# The goose has a bill.

# The goose is soft.

# The goose gets in
# the lake.

God made the goose.

God made the moose.

# The moose is big!

# Do you see her big nose?

# The moose has four long legs.

# The moose has big horns.

# Horns are
# antlers (ANT-lers).

God made the moose.

God made the
mongoose.

The mongoose has
a long face.

# The mongoose has a long tail.

A mongoose has small ears and short legs.

# A mongoose can kill a snake.

# God made the mongoose.

God made the goose,
moose, and mongoose

# God made them all.

God made them all on
days five and six.

# God is good!

# The "Learn to Read" Series: A Word to Parents

**Rationale:** To provide books for children (ages 3-6) from Christian homes for the purpose of assisting them in **learning to read** while simultaneously introducing them to the **Creator** and His **creation.**

## Difficulty Level

The following listing provides a breakdown of the number and length of words in *Goose, Moose, and Mongoose* (not counting plurals and duplicates):

## Total Number of Words: 44

**1—One letter word**
a

**4—Two letters words**
is, in, do, on

**17—Three letter words**
God, the, big, has, leg, can, fly, you,
her, get, ear, and, are, all, day, six, see

**15—Four letter words**
made, nose, four, long, horn,
bird, soft, bill, lake, tail, five,
face, kill, them, good

**5—Five letter words**
goose, moose, small, short, snake

**1—Six letter word**
antler

**1—Eight letter word**
mongoose

**Drawings by**
**Alanna Hallenbeck, Age 10**

# The A.P. Readers

## LEVEL 1
### "Learn to Read"

1. Dogs, Frogs, and Hogs
2. Bats, Cats, and Rats
3. Birds, Bugs, and Bees
4. Fish, Flies, and Fleas
5. Goose, Moose, and Mongoose
6. Ducks, Bucks, and Woodchucks

## LEVEL 2
### "Early Reader"

1. God Made the World
2. God Made Dinosaurs
3. God Made Animals
4. God Made Insects
5. God Made Plants
6. God Made Fish

## LEVEL 3
### "Advanced Reader"

Coming Soon!

We are continuing to expand the number of titles in each series. Be sure to check our Web site for our newest books.
www.ApologeticsPress.org